PENGUIN moves out of the ANTARCTIC

T0084479

by Nikki Potts • illustrated by Maarten Lenoir

PICTURE WINDOW BOOKS
a capstone imprint

Fish, fish, and more fish!

Penguin is sick of eating fish.

White, white, and
more white!

Penguin is sick of all the white.

Everything is cold
in the Antarctic.

Everything is hard
and icy. Penguin
wants a change.

ICEBERGS
EVERYWHERE
BRRR!

ZOOOOM!
Penguin slides into
a soft, sandy paradise.

OUCH!
Sand is not the same as ice!

WHOOSH!

A long-eared jackrabbit darts by.
Look out, Penguin!

Tired and hot,
Penguin looks for
a place to rest.

YIKES!

The chairs here are
a little sharp.

Under a large banana tree,
Penguin finds some shade.

He is not used
to the heat!

Ssssssss . . . uddenly,
a snake slithers by.

Penguin wasn't looking
for a new neighbor!

Penguin waddles away as
fast as his flippers can go.

He finds a quiet pond
where he can be alone.

Time for a swim!

Penguin is looking
forward to jumping in.

He has **really** missed water!

SHALLOW

PLOP!

But ponds aren't as deep as the ocean.

Disappointed, Penguin waves
his flippers in the air.

The pond is too shallow.

He can't float.
He can't even get up!

Penguin thinks and thinks.
None of these new places
feel like home.

Where else can he go?

If you liked...
You'll love...

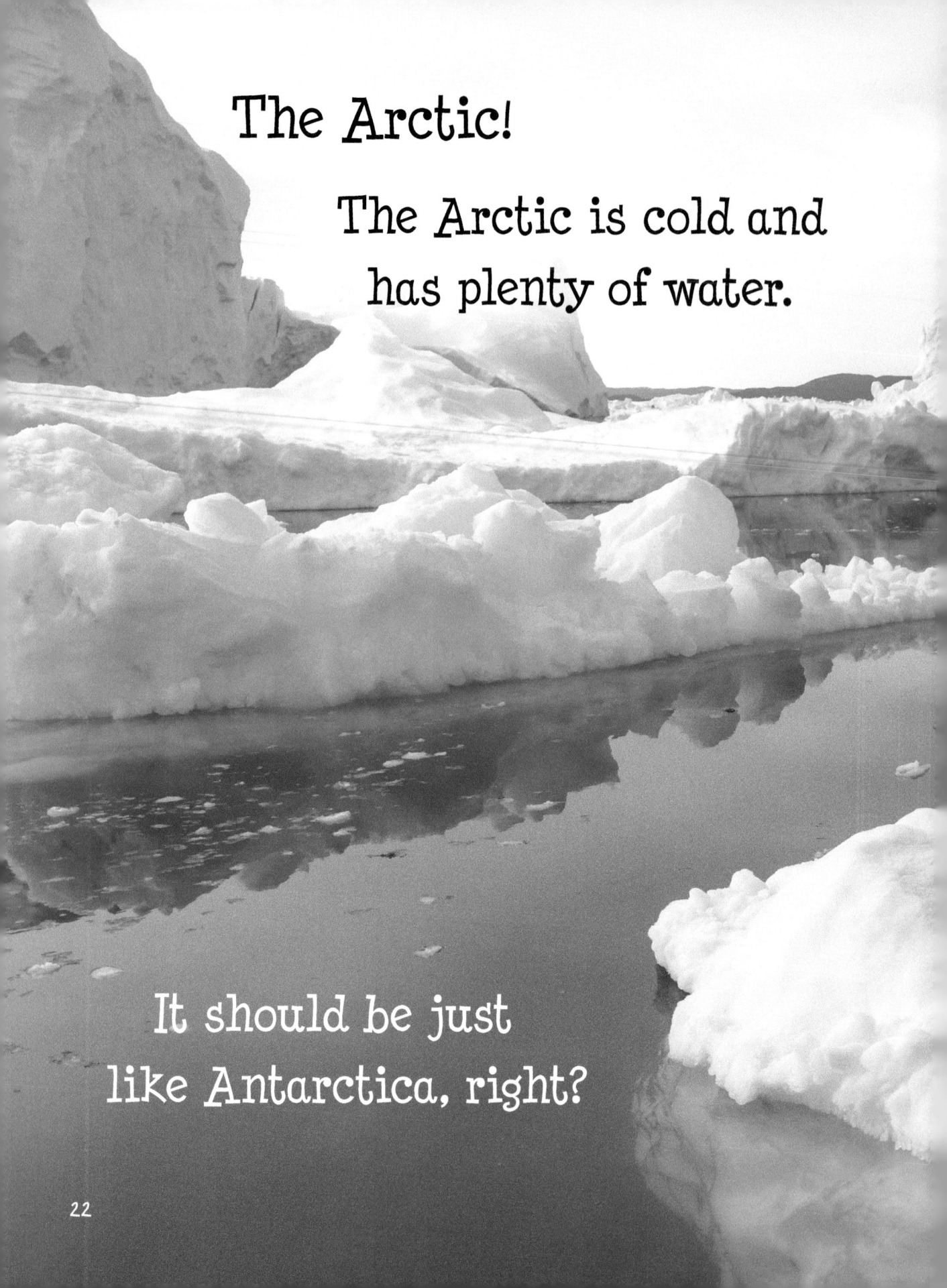

The Arctic!

The Arctic is cold and has plenty of water.

It should be just like Antarctica, right?

Grrrrrr!

Or maybe not!
A giant polar bear charges!

Penguin drops to his belly.

He zips to
the ocean
just in
time.

Home at last!

Penguin thinks that maybe his home is pretty nice after all.

It's cold. There is lots of water. He has plenty of friends.

There are no scary snakes or bears!

Welcome home, Penguin!

And the fish aren't
so bad after all.

MORE ABOUT EMPEROR PENGUINS

Although emperor penguins are birds, they can't fly.

Females lay one egg and then leave to hunt. They come back with food after about two months. The male cares for the egg until the chick hatches.

They are the largest penguin species.

Emperor penguins have four layers of waterproof feathers. Feathers help keep the penguins warm.

Strong claws on their feet help emperor penguins move on the slippery ice.

Emperor penguins can eat up to 11 pounds (5 kilograms) of food per day.